SELF-CARE JOURNAL: DAILY CHECK-IN

SELF-CARE
JOURNAL
DAILY CHECK-IN

75 Days of Reflection Space to Track Your Self-Care Practice

ALEXA BRAND, LMFT

ROCKRIDGE PRESS

Interior and Cover Designer: Jane Archer
Art Producer: Melissa Malinowsky
Editor: Eun H. Jeong
Production Editor: Caroline Flanagan
Production Manager: Jose Olivera

Copyright Page: © Geometrica Bureau/Creative Market, cover; All other illustrations used under license from kloroform/Creative Market.

Paperback ISBN: 978-1-63807-687-2
R0

THIS JOURNAL BELONGS TO:

_____

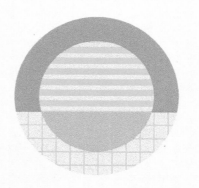

CONTENTS

INTRODUCTION

Self-care didn't come naturally to me growing up. It felt easy for me to take care of others and wrong for me to take care of myself. I wanted to be selfless, not selfish—so much so that I hadn't nourished a relationship with myself and barely knew who I was. The concept of taking care of myself felt distant and even scary.

Furthermore, self-care activities had become twisted in my mind due to unhealthy messages in the media. Physical activity became a form of retribution for being overweight. Calorie-dense food became "bad." To take a nap was to be "lazy." Self-care was presented as punishing. There was no gentle approach to taking care of myself. Thankfully, I began therapy and started to unlearn these toxic messages.

Through true, compassionate self-care, I began to heal and thrive beyond what I ever thought was possible. True self-care is medicine for our bodies, minds, and souls. Self-care isn't selfish. It is a chance for us to reconnect with our authentic selves and values.

I am now a licensed therapist who specializes in self-compassion. It is my life's purpose to help others find their own self-care path. That's why I created this journal for you, to help you wherever you are in your journey.

Here's to cultivating more kindness, well-being, and joy in your life!

I am **worthy** of receiving the same kindness and attention that I give to others.

PART I

What Is Self-Care?

More than Naps and Meditation

The term "self-care" is thrown around a lot. In fact, you may have a specific idea of what self-care is supposed to be. This section will help you open your mind to all that self-care can be.

Let's start with a basic definition. Self-care is the act of promoting well-being and health within oneself through thoughtful action. It's very important to clarify that true self-care is also compassionate. This means that self-care acts are kind, forgiving, and understanding of your specific needs. Self-care soothes and isn't a punishment. It's also not about being perfect. True self-care moves gently through obstacles that may arise. This may seem obvious to you. But for those who pursue perfection, it's an important reminder and a key aspect of healthy self-care.

Furthermore, self-care is personal and individualized. Self-care is whatever *you* deem is necessary to support a healthy, adaptive lifestyle for *you*. Self-care is about authenticity, flexibility, and nourishment. Therefore, it is critical for you to build a self-care routine that aligns with *your* lifestyle, values, and personality. Self-care that works for one person may not work for you at all. Meet yourself where you are. Stay true to your own needs in this process.

The Importance of Self-Care

Research has found that self-care increases overall well-being, lowers morbidity rates, decreases stress levels, and even impacts mortality. This means self-care is literally connected to your lifeline!

It is important to have a diverse set of self-care practices because different types of self-care nourish different areas. Physical self-care improves your body's health. This may look like setting up the dentist appointment you've been putting off or finding joyful activities that allow your body to get moving. Mental self-care positively impacts your mental health. This may look like practicing daily positive affirmations or going to a weekly support group. Soulful or spiritual self-care nurtures your inner self. This may look like taking a walk in nature or watching your favorite comedy. There are many different ways you can practice beneficial self-care.

Additionally, your self-care puts you in a better place to help others, as you model healthy skills to those around you. Your act of self-care is like a ripple on a pond—one act causes a chain reaction that benefits those around you. For example, if you have children, modeling self-care shows them it's okay for them to take care of themselves and that self-care isn't selfish. Self-care is not only vital for you to flourish, but also for your loved ones and community.

Signs to Slow Down

Beware of burnout! Burnout is your body's way of telling you that you are doing too much—mentally, physically, and spiritually. Symptoms of burnout are feeling drained, fatigued, irritable, sad, unbalanced, and/or anxious. Burnout can appear as somatic, or physical, symptoms, such as headaches, body aches, and tension. Burnout can also show up in your behaviors. Perhaps you isolate yourself or do not find pleasure in doing things you normally enjoy.

When you notice the signs and symptoms of burnout, it's time to reflect on your schedule and embrace some much-needed self-care. Ironically, sometimes engaging in a lot of self-care activities can also lead to burnout. Self-care may actually mean taking some downtime to rest. Rest is restorative! Do your best to continually analyze your lifestyle and self-care routine and make compassionate modifications and adjustments as needed.

Rituals to Reach Goals

Creating healthy routines around your self-care is an incredible restoration tool for burnout—meaning it can help you refuel when you're running on empty! And not only that, self-care is also a preventive tool *to* burnout. This means that creating manageable daily/weekly/monthly/yearly self-care rituals will help decrease the likelihood that you'll reach burnout. Creating timely, structured self-care habits is vital to developing sustainable, long-term health and is extremely beneficial for your well-being. You will maintain greater balance in your life and have more opportunities to achieve your goals! It's important to note that it may take some time to find consistency and balance in these self-care rituals. That's why it's so important to hold compassion for yourself in the process.

You may be wondering where to start. To begin, try brainstorming your values and aligned (authentic to yourself) self-care goals. Figure out what your intentions are with self-care to create specific goals. Also, make sure your self-care routines and goals are developed from a place of self-compassion rather than from your inner critic (the self-critical part of you). With self-compassion at the wheel, you will increase motivation and be significantly more likely to reach your self-care goals. Need some inspiration? Here are some basic self-care activities that are helpful for many people:

Sleep maintenance—Getting seven to eight hours of sleep per night can improve one's mood. Logging when you go to bed and wake up can help you gain insight into your sleep patterns.

Daily gratitude practice—Finding one thing to appreciate each day can help rewire your brain to focus more on the positive and simultaneously boost your mood.

Mood tracker—Identifying your overall mood for the day, as well as the lows and highs of your day, can help you increase awareness of your emotions, making you better prepared to take compassionate action.

Keep in mind, these are just starting points. You can make your rituals specific to your own needs.

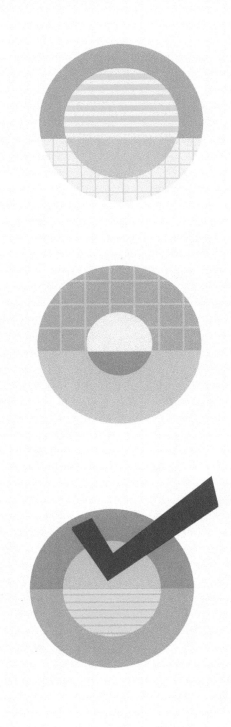

I am
healing myself
through actions that
nourish my body,
mind, and spirit.

PART II

Self-Care Tracking and Journaling

Reflecting on Self-Care

The tracker and tools in this journal will guide you in learning more about your relationship to self-care. You will keep tabs on your daily self-care rituals, moods, energy levels, and goals and intentions in order to reflect on your self-care. You will answer thought-provoking questions that will help you gain insight into your specific self-care needs. You will also be provided with exercises and self-care tips to aid you on your self-care journey.

Try to use each part of this journal to help you identify the routines and rituals that are beneficial to you, the ones that are not helpful, and the ones that are life-changing so you can build a self-care routine that is right for you. Remember, you can modify and change your self-care routine at any time. In fact, you are encouraged to do so on this journey, as it is highly likely that your needs will change as your life does. Also, what works for another person may not work for you, so don't be afraid to modify common self-care practices to meet your own needs. Remember, flexibility and kindness are key!

Baseline Check-In

Before you begin using this journal, it is important to identify where you are currently in your self-care journey. This is called your baseline. Your baseline is used to help you identify appropriate self-care goals. Without knowing your baseline, you may set goals that are too high or too low, and this could lead to disappointment or fatigue. Identifying your baseline will help you be realistic in your goal setting. Meeting yourself where you are will lead to more success in the long run.

Answer the following questions to help you identify your self-care baseline:

1. What self-care practices are you following now that have provided a positive impact?

_____

_____

_____

2. What self-care practices have you followed in the past, but no longer benefit you?

_____

_____

_____

3. Do you currently engage in some types of self-care but not others? If so, describe them. (For example, you have an exercise routine for physical health but no self-care routine for mental health.)

_____

_____

_____

4. What parts of your life could benefit from more nourishment?

_____

_____

_____

Goals

You've established your self-care baseline. Now it's time to identify some self-care goals! It's helpful to begin by reflecting on your current lifestyle, values, personality traits, and cultural background. This will ensure that your goals are individualized to your specific interests and needs.

1. What kind of lifestyle do you have? *(Check all boxes that apply.)*

☐ Academic ☐ Minimalist

☐ Activist ☐ Religious

☐ Corporate ☐ Slow-paced

☐ Creative ☐ Spiritual

☐ Digital ☐ Sustainable

☐ Fast-paced ☐ Workaholic

☐ Materialistic ☐ Other _____

2. What values resonate with you? *(Check all boxes that apply.)*

☐ Adventure ☐ Freedom

☐ Authenticity ☐ Healing

☐ Balance ☐ Health

☐ Community ☐ Intelligence

☐ Connection ☐ Joy

☐ Consciousness ☐ Spirituality

☐ Creativity ☐ Vitality

☐ Development ☐ Other _____

☐ Efficiency

☐ Equity

☐ Fitness

3. What personality traits do you have? *(Check all boxes that apply.)*

☐ Adventurous

☐ Ambitious

☐ Analytical

☐ Anxious

☐ Assertive

☐ Calm

☐ Cautious

☐ Clever

☐ Competitive

☐ Emotional

☐ Empath

☐ Extrovert

☐ Flexible

☐ Focused

☐ Highly sensitive

☐ Impatient

☐ Introvert

☐ Logical

☐ Modest

☐ Moody

☐ Organized

☐ Perfectionist

☐ Selfish

☐ Selfless

☐ Type A

☐ Other _____

4. What is your cultural background?

- **Gender identity:** _____

- **Sexual orientation:** _____

- **Race/ethnicity:** _____

- **Age:** _____

- **Socioeconomic status:** _____

- **Spirituality/religion:** _____

Now, using your baseline and lifestyle reflections, begin to brainstorm some intentions (areas of focus) and self-care goals you hope to achieve in your life. It's important not to set goals that are too challenging or too easy. Doing so will likely leave you feeling disappointed and lower your overall motivation. Start with manageable goals. Also, these goals should not be developed from a self-critical or punishment mindset, but rather a kind, self-compassionate one. You will be more likely to stick with your goals if you have a caring mindset!

1. What self-care goals do you hope to accomplish?

_____

_____

_____

2. How do you see these goals manifesting?

_____

_____

_____

3. What habits, rituals, and routines can you embrace to help you achieve these self-care goals?

_____

_____

_____

How to Use This Journal

In part III (see page 17) of this journal, you will find 75 days of trackers, prompts, tips, and exercises to help you build, track, and expand on your self-care and reach your self-care goals.

Begin each day by filling out the Morning Check-In section. This will help you start your day with a self-care mindset. You don't have to fill in everything, but do try to challenge yourself to complete as much as you can.

MORNING CHECK-IN:

Sleep—Identify what time you went to sleep the night before and what time you woke up. Add up how many hours you slept that night.

Morning mood—Track your morning mood by circling one of the emojis.

Energy level—Track how much energy your body has: low, medium or high.

Daily goals—Identify three manageable goals for your day. For example, you might decide to take a meaningful walk.

Today's affirmation or intention—Identify a positive affirmation for your day. For example, you might decide to say to yourself, "I am resilient." Or you may identify something that you want to focus on throughout your day. For example, you might write in your journal or say to yourself: "Notice moments of joy."

In the evening, complete the Evening Reflection section. This will help you contemplate the ways you embraced self-care, made it your own, and help you evaluate your progress.

EVENING REFLECTION:

Evening mood—Track your evening mood by circling one of the emojis.

Energy level—Track how much energy your body has: low, medium or high.

Self-care—Check off the self-care activities you engaged in and add your own.

How did I embrace self-compassion today?—Identify ways that you were kind and understanding toward yourself. For example, perhaps you forgave yourself for perceived mistakes you made at work.

What is a challenge I overcame through self-care today?—Identify a setback or a moment of hardship you overcame. For example, maybe you practiced deep breathing when you felt overwhelmed.

At any time of the day, you may turn to the **Reflective Prompt**, **Tips and Tricks**, or **Exercise** sections. These tools will help you dive deeper into your self-care lifestyle and modify it as needed. The Reflective Prompts can help you gain insight into your relationship with self-care. The Tips and Tricks provide handy strategies to help you reach your self-care goals. The Exercises offer self-care practices you can add to your self-care regimen as you see fit.

It's time to spread your wings and start tracking! Remember, hold compassion for yourself on this self-care journey—and know that you can do it!

Today, I will treat myself with **deep care** and **compassion.**

PART III

75 Daily Trackers

DAILY TRACKER

MORNING CHECK-IN

MOOD:

ENERGY LEVEL: 🔋 🔋 🔋

SLEEP:

FROM: _____ a.m./p.m.

TO: _____ a.m./p.m.

TOTAL: _____ hours

DAILY GOALS:

1. _____
2. _____
3. _____

AFFIRMATION OR INTENTION:

_____
_____
_____
_____
_____

EVENING REFLECTION

MOOD: ☺ ☺ 😆

ENERGY LEVEL: 🔋 🔋 🔋

SELF-CARE:

○ Shower/Bath   ○ Gratitude
○ Meditation   ○ Quiet time
○ Journaling   ○ Fun time
○ Joyful movement   ○ Mindful eating
○ Reading   ○ Goal work
○ _____
○ _____
○ _____

How did I embrace self-compassion today?

_____
_____

What is a challenge I overcame through self-care today?

_____
_____
_____

REFLECTIVE PROMPT

Why is it important for you to step out of your comfort zone? What do you hope to achieve?

DAILY TRACKER

MORNING CHECK-IN

MOOD: 😊 😆

ENERGY LEVEL: 🔋 🔋 🔋

SLEEP:

FROM: _____ a.m./p.m.

TO: _____ a.m./p.m.

TOTAL: _____ hours

DAILY GOALS:

1. _____

2. _____

3. _____

AFFIRMATION OR INTENTION:

_____

_____

_____

_____

_____

EVENING REFLECTION

MOOD: 😟 🤬 😐 😊 😆

ENERGY LEVEL: 🔋 🔋 🔋

SELF-CARE:

○ Shower/Bath　　○ Gratitude
○ Meditation　　　○ Quiet time
○ Journaling　　　○ Fun time
○ Joyful movement　○ Mindful eating
○ Reading　　　　○ Goal work

○ _____

○ _____

○ _____

How did I embrace self-compassion today?

_____

_____

_____

What is a challenge I overcame through self-care today?

_____

_____

_____

_____

TIPS AND TRICKS

Schedule in rest time. That's right, literally schedule it in your calendar. Next, set an alert on your phone (or other device) to pop up when it is time to rest. Write down any resistance you felt to scheduling in rest. Then identify one reason scheduling in rest will foster self-care.

DAILY TRACKER

MORNING CHECK-IN

MOOD:

ENERGY LEVEL: 🔋 🔋 🔋

SLEEP:

FROM: _____ a.m./p.m.

TO: _____ a.m./p.m.

TOTAL: _____ hours

DAILY GOALS:

1. _____

2. _____

3. _____

AFFIRMATION OR INTENTION:

_____

_____

_____

_____

_____

EVENING REFLECTION

MOOD: 😞 😭 😐 😊 😆

ENERGY LEVEL: 🔋 🔋 🔋

SELF-CARE:

○ Shower/Bath   ○ Gratitude
○ Meditation   ○ Quiet time
○ Journaling   ○ Fun time
○ Joyful movement   ○ Mindful eating
○ Reading   ○ Goal work
○ _____
○ _____
○ _____

How did I embrace self-compassion today?

_____

_____

What is a challenge I overcame through self-care today?

_____

_____

_____

REFLECTIVE PROMPT

Identify one moment when you were hard on yourself today. How can you embrace self-compassion to help you through these moments in the future?

DAILY TRACKER

MORNING CHECK-IN

MOOD: 😄

ENERGY LEVEL: 🔋 🔋 🔋

SLEEP:

FROM: _____ a.m./p.m.

TO: _____ a.m./p.m.

TOTAL: _____ hours

DAILY GOALS:

1. _____

2. _____

3. _____

AFFIRMATION OR INTENTION:

_____

_____

_____

_____

_____

EVENING REFLECTION

MOOD: ☺️ 😄

ENERGY LEVEL: 🔋 🔋 🔋

SELF-CARE:

- ○ Shower/Bath
- ○ Meditation
- ○ Journaling
- ○ Joyful movement
- ○ Reading
- ○ Gratitude
- ○ Quiet time
- ○ Fun time
- ○ Mindful eating
- ○ Goal work

○ _____

○ _____

○ _____

How did I embrace self-compassion today?

_____

_____

What is a challenge I overcame through self-care today?

_____

_____

_____

REFLECTIVE PROMPT

What boundaries have you or do you need to set to ensure your self-care journey blossoms and endures?

DAILY TRACKER

MORNING CHECK-IN

MOOD:

ENERGY LEVEL: 🔋 🔋 🔋

SLEEP:

FROM: _____ a.m./p.m.

TO: _____ a.m./p.m.

TOTAL: _____ hours

DAILY GOALS:

1. _____

2. _____

3. _____

AFFIRMATION OR INTENTION:

_____

_____

_____

_____

_____

EVENING REFLECTION

MOOD:

ENERGY LEVEL: 🔋 🔋 🔋

SELF-CARE:

- ○ Shower/Bath
- ○ Meditation
- ○ Journaling
- ○ Joyful movement
- ○ Reading
- ○ Gratitude
- ○ Quiet time
- ○ Fun time
- ○ Mindful eating
- ○ Goal work

○ _____

○ _____

○ _____

How did I embrace self-compassion today?

_____

_____

What is a challenge I overcame through self-care today?

_____

_____

EXERCISE

Close your eyes and repeat the mantra "I am worthy of good things" 10 times. Take note of any shifts in your mood or in your body. Record these shifts or any forms of resistance you feel.

DAILY TRACKER

MORNING CHECK-IN

MOOD:

ENERGY LEVEL: 🔋 🔋 🔋

SLEEP:

FROM: _____ a.m./p.m.

TO: _____ a.m./p.m.

TOTAL: _____ hours

DAILY GOALS:

1. _____

2. _____

3. _____

AFFIRMATION OR INTENTION:

_____

_____

_____

_____

_____

EVENING REFLECTION

MOOD:

ENERGY LEVEL: 🔋 🔋 🔋

SELF-CARE:

○ Shower/Bath   ○ Gratitude
○ Meditation   ○ Quiet time
○ Journaling   ○ Fun time
○ Joyful movement ○ Mindful eating
○ Reading   ○ Goal work
○ _____
○ _____
○ _____

How did I embrace self-compassion today?

_____

_____

What is a challenge I overcame through self-care today?

_____

_____

REFLECTIVE PROMPT

Identify your ideal environment for feeling calm (e.g., nature, bed-room, beach). What factors make this the ideal environment (e.g., sounds, colors, people, smells)?

DAILY TRACKER

MORNING CHECK-IN

MOOD:

ENERGY LEVEL: 🔋 🔋 🔋

SLEEP:

FROM: _____ a.m./p.m.

TO: _____ a.m./p.m.

TOTAL: _____ hours

DAILY GOALS:

1. _____
2. _____
3. _____

AFFIRMATION OR INTENTION:

_____
_____
_____
_____
_____

EVENING REFLECTION

MOOD: ☺ ☺ ☺

ENERGY LEVEL: 🔋 🔋 🔋

SELF-CARE:

- ○ Shower/Bath
- ○ Meditation
- ○ Journaling
- ○ Joyful movement
- ○ Reading
- ○ Gratitude
- ○ Quiet time
- ○ Fun time
- ○ Mindful eating
- ○ Goal work

○ _____

○ _____

○ _____

How did I embrace self-compassion today?

_____
_____

What is a challenge I overcame through self-care today?

_____
_____
_____

REFLECTIVE PROMPT

What parts of yourself are asking for more attention? How can you show those parts more care?

_____

_____

_____

_____

_____

_____

_____

_____

_____

_____

_____

_____

_____

_____

_____

_____

_____

DAILY TRACKER

MORNING CHECK-IN

MOOD: ☺ 😆

ENERGY LEVEL: 🔋 🔋 🔋

SLEEP:

FROM: _____ a.m./p.m.

TO: _____ a.m./p.m.

TOTAL: _____ hours

DAILY GOALS:

1. _____

2. _____

3. _____

AFFIRMATION OR INTENTION:

_____

_____

_____

_____

_____

EVENING REFLECTION

MOOD: ☹   ☺ 😆

ENERGY LEVEL: 🔋 🔋 🔋

SELF-CARE:

○ Shower/Bath   ○ Gratitude

○ Meditation   ○ Quiet time

○ Journaling   ○ Fun time

○ Joyful movement   ○ Mindful eating

○ Reading   ○ Goal work

○ _____

○ _____

○ _____

How did I embrace self-compassion today?

_____

_____

What is a challenge I overcame through self-care today?

_____

_____

_____

REFLECTIVE PROMPT

The more you resist challenges, the more they will persist in your mind. What is one thing you've been resisting lately? How can you move toward more acceptance?

DAILY TRACKER

MORNING CHECK-IN

MOOD: 😆

ENERGY LEVEL: 🔋 🔋 🔋

SLEEP:

FROM: _____ a.m./p.m.

TO: _____ a.m./p.m.

TOTAL: _____ hours

DAILY GOALS:

1. _____

2. _____

3. _____

AFFIRMATION OR INTENTION:

_____
_____
_____
_____
_____
_____

EVENING REFLECTION

MOOD: ☺ 😊 😆

ENERGY LEVEL: 🔋 🔋 🔋

SELF-CARE:

○ Shower/Bath   ○ Gratitude

○ Meditation   ○ Quiet time

○ Journaling   ○ Fun time

○ Joyful movement ○ Mindful eating

○ Reading   ○ Goal work

○ _____

○ _____

○ _____

How did I embrace self-compassion today?

_____
_____
_____

What is a challenge I overcame through self-care today?

_____
_____
_____

TIPS AND TRICKS

Embrace 30 seconds of stillness. Sometimes we have days when we can't catch a break. Find 30 seconds and just be still. Focus on your breath or listen to the sounds around you. Even 30 seconds of stillness is self-care. How do moments of stillness impact you?

DAILY TRACKER

MORNING CHECK-IN

MOOD: 😊 😄

ENERGY LEVEL: 🔋 🔋 🔋

SLEEP:

FROM: _____ a.m./p.m.

TO: _____ a.m./p.m.

TOTAL: _____ hours

DAILY GOALS:

1. _____

2. _____

3. _____

AFFIRMATION OR INTENTION:

_____

_____

_____

_____

_____

EVENING REFLECTION

MOOD: 😄

ENERGY LEVEL: 🔋 🔋 🔋

SELF-CARE:

- ○ Shower/Bath
- ○ Meditation
- ○ Journaling
- ○ Joyful movement
- ○ Reading

- ○ Gratitude
- ○ Quiet time
- ○ Fun time
- ○ Mindful eating
- ○ Goal work

○ _____

○ _____

○ _____

How did I embrace self-compassion today?

_____

_____

_____

What is a challenge I overcame through self-care today?

_____

_____

_____

REFLECTIVE PROMPT

What is something you want to stop doing that no longer serves you? What can you put in its place?

_____

_____

_____

_____

_____

_____

_____

_____

_____

_____

_____

_____

_____

_____

_____

_____

_____

_____

DAILY TRACKER

MORNING CHECK-IN

MOOD:

ENERGY LEVEL: 🔋 🔋 🔋

SLEEP:

FROM: _____ a.m./p.m.

TO: _____ a.m./p.m.

TOTAL: _____ hours

DAILY GOALS:

1. _____

2. _____

3. _____

AFFIRMATION OR INTENTION:

_____

_____

_____

_____

_____

EVENING REFLECTION

MOOD:

ENERGY LEVEL: 🔋 🔋 🔋

SELF-CARE:

○ Shower/Bath   ○ Gratitude
○ Meditation   ○ Quiet time
○ Journaling   ○ Fun time
○ Joyful movement   ○ Mindful eating
○ Reading   ○ Goal work

○ _____

○ _____

○ _____

How did I embrace self-compassion today?

_____

_____

_____

What is a challenge I overcame through self-care today?

_____

_____

_____

REFLECTIVE PROMPT

What are some of the ways that you've depleted your energy and neglected your self-care in the past?

_____

_____

_____

_____

_____

_____

_____

_____

_____

_____

_____

_____

_____

_____

_____

_____

DAILY TRACKER

MORNING CHECK-IN

MOOD:

ENERGY LEVEL: 🔋 🔋 🔋

SLEEP:

FROM: _____ a.m./p.m.

TO: _____ a.m./p.m.

TOTAL: _____ hours

DAILY GOALS:

1. _____

2. _____

3. _____

AFFIRMATION OR INTENTION:

_____
_____
_____
_____
_____

EVENING REFLECTION

MOOD: ☹ 😭 😐 🙂 😄

ENERGY LEVEL: 🔋 🔋 🔋

SELF-CARE:

○ Shower/Bath   ○ Gratitude
○ Meditation   ○ Quiet time
○ Journaling   ○ Fun time
○ Joyful movement   ○ Mindful eating
○ Reading   ○ Goal work

○ _____
○ _____
○ _____

How did I embrace self-compassion today?

_____
_____
_____

What is a challenge I overcame through self-care today?

_____
_____
_____

TIPS AND TRICKS

Foster a curious mindset about exercise. Ask yourself what types of physical activity bring you joy. You are far more likely to keep up an exercise regimen when you enjoy what you are doing. Write down the types of movement that bring you joy.

DAILY TRACKER

MORNING CHECK-IN

MOOD:

ENERGY LEVEL:

SLEEP:

FROM: _____ a.m./p.m.

TO: _____ a.m./p.m.

TOTAL: _____ hours

DAILY GOALS:

1. _____

2. _____

3. _____

AFFIRMATION OR INTENTION:

_____

_____

_____

_____

_____

EVENING REFLECTION

MOOD:

ENERGY LEVEL:

SELF-CARE:

- ○ Shower/Bath
- ○ Meditation
- ○ Journaling
- ○ Joyful movement
- ○ Reading
- ○ Gratitude
- ○ Quiet time
- ○ Fun time
- ○ Mindful eating
- ○ Goal work

○ _____

○ _____

○ _____

How did I embrace self-compassion today?

_____

_____

_____

What is a challenge I overcame through self-care today?

_____

_____

_____

REFLECTIVE PROMPT

When do you feel like your most authentic self? What allows you to feel this way in those moments?

_____

_____

_____

_____

_____

_____

_____

_____

_____

_____

_____

_____

_____

_____

_____

_____

_____

_____

DAILY TRACKER

MORNING CHECK-IN	EVENING REFLECTION

MORNING CHECK-IN

MOOD:

ENERGY LEVEL: 🔋 🔋 🔋

SLEEP:

FROM: _____ a.m./p.m.

TO: _____ a.m./p.m.

TOTAL: _____ hours

DAILY GOALS:

1. _____

2. _____

3. _____

AFFIRMATION OR INTENTION:

_____

_____

_____

_____

_____

EVENING REFLECTION

MOOD:

ENERGY LEVEL: 🔋 🔋 🔋

SELF-CARE:

- ○ Shower/Bath
- ○ Meditation
- ○ Journaling
- ○ Joyful movement
- ○ Reading
- ○ Gratitude
- ○ Quiet time
- ○ Fun time
- ○ Mindful eating
- ○ Goal work
- ○ _____
- ○ _____
- ○ _____

How did I embrace self-compassion today?

_____

_____

What is a challenge I overcame through self-care today?

_____

_____

REFLECTIVE PROMPT

If you are on the go and don't have much time for yourself, what are some easy ways that you can engage in quick self-care?

DAILY TRACKER

MORNING CHECK-IN	EVENING REFLECTION

MOOD: ☺ 😄

MOOD: 😖 😭 😐 ☺ 😄

ENERGY LEVEL: 🔋 🔋 🔋

ENERGY LEVEL: 🔋 🔋 🔋

SLEEP:

FROM: _____ a.m./p.m.

TO: _____ a.m./p.m.

TOTAL: _____ hours

DAILY GOALS:

1. _____

2. _____

3. _____

AFFIRMATION OR INTENTION:

_____

_____

_____

_____

_____

_____

SELF-CARE:

○ Shower/Bath   ○ Gratitude

○ Meditation   ○ Quiet time

○ Journaling   ○ Fun time

○ Joyful movement ○ Mindful eating

○ Reading   ○ Goal work

○ _____

○ _____

○ _____

How did I embrace self-compassion today?

_____

_____

What is a challenge I overcame through self-care today?

_____

_____

REFLECTIVE PROMPT

What are some ways that you have begun prioritizing your self-care? If you haven't been able to, what has held you back?

DAILY TRACKER

MORNING CHECK-IN

MOOD: 😄

ENERGY LEVEL: 🔋 🔋 🔋

SLEEP:

FROM: _____ a.m./p.m.

TO: _____ a.m./p.m.

TOTAL: _____ hours

DAILY GOALS:

1. _____

2. _____

3. _____

AFFIRMATION OR INTENTION:

_____

_____

_____

_____

EVENING REFLECTION

MOOD: 😊 😄

ENERGY LEVEL: 🔋 🔋 🔋

SELF-CARE:

- ○ Shower/Bath
- ○ Meditation
- ○ Journaling
- ○ Joyful movement
- ○ Reading
- ○ Gratitude
- ○ Quiet time
- ○ Fun time
- ○ Mindful eating
- ○ Goal work
- ○ _____
- ○ _____
- ○ _____

How did I embrace self-compassion today?

_____

_____

What is a challenge I overcame through self-care today?

_____

_____

_____

EXERCISE

Check in with how your body feels. If comfortable, engage the muscles in your body by gently squeezing them all at once. Hold the squeeze for five in-and-out breaths. Release your muscles on the fifth out breath. Notice the physical sensations that show up as you release. How does your body feel after this exercise?

DAILY TRACKER

MORNING CHECK-IN

MOOD:

ENERGY LEVEL: 🔋 🔋 🔋

SLEEP:

FROM: _____ a.m./p.m.

TO: _____ a.m./p.m.

TOTAL: _____ hours

DAILY GOALS:

1. _____
2. _____
3. _____

AFFIRMATION OR INTENTION:

_____

_____

_____

_____

_____

_____

EVENING REFLECTION

MOOD:

ENERGY LEVEL: 🔋 🔋 🔋

SELF-CARE:

○ Shower/Bath   ○ Gratitude
○ Meditation   ○ Quiet time
○ Journaling   ○ Fun time
○ Joyful movement ○ Mindful eating
○ Reading   ○ Goal work
○ _____
○ _____
○ _____

How did I embrace self-compassion today?

_____

_____

What is a challenge I overcame through self-care today?

_____

_____

REFLECTIVE PROMPT

Where and when do you feel most connected to the universe?

DAILY TRACKER

MORNING CHECK-IN

EVENING REFLECTION

MOOD: ☺ 😄

MOOD: 😟 ☺ ☺ 😄

ENERGY LEVEL: 🔋 🔋 🔋

ENERGY LEVEL: 🔋 🔋 🔋

SLEEP:

FROM: _____ a.m./p.m.

TO: _____ a.m./p.m.

TOTAL: _____ hours

SELF-CARE:

○ Shower/Bath   ○ Gratitude
○ Meditation   ○ Quiet time
○ Journaling   ○ Fun time
○ Joyful movement   ○ Mindful eating
○ Reading   ○ Goal work
○ _____
○ _____
○ _____

How did I embrace self-compassion today?

_____
_____
_____

DAILY GOALS:

1. _____
2. _____
3. _____

AFFIRMATION OR INTENTION:

_____
_____
_____
_____
_____

What is a challenge I overcame through self-care today?

_____
_____
_____

REFLECTIVE PROMPT

How can you begin to listen more to your body's needs? What specific actions can you take to address those needs?

DAILY TRACKER

MORNING CHECK-IN

MOOD:

ENERGY LEVEL:

SLEEP:

FROM: _____ a.m./p.m.

TO: _____ a.m./p.m.

TOTAL: _____ hours

DAILY GOALS:

1. _____
2. _____
3. _____

AFFIRMATION OR INTENTION:

_____

_____

_____

_____

_____

EVENING REFLECTION

MOOD:

ENERGY LEVEL:

SELF-CARE:

○ Shower/Bath   ○ Gratitude
○ Meditation   ○ Quiet time
○ Journaling   ○ Fun time
○ Joyful movement ○ Mindful eating
○ Reading   ○ Goal work
○ _____
○ _____
○ _____

How did I embrace self-compassion today?

_____

_____

_____

What is a challenge I overcame through self-care today?

_____

_____

_____

REFLECTIVE PROMPT

In what ways did you display resilience today? Remember, sometimes resilience means just getting through the day!

DAILY TRACKER

MORNING CHECK-IN

MOOD: ☹ 😖 😐 🙂 😄

ENERGY LEVEL: 🔋 🔋 🔋

SLEEP:

FROM: _____ a.m./p.m.

TO: _____ a.m./p.m.

TOTAL: _____ hours

DAILY GOALS:

1. _____
2. _____
3. _____

AFFIRMATION OR INTENTION:

_____
_____
_____
_____
_____
_____

EVENING REFLECTION

MOOD: ☹ 😖 😐 🙂 😄

ENERGY LEVEL: 🔋 🔋 🔋

SELF-CARE:

- ◯ Shower/Bath
- ◯ Meditation
- ◯ Journaling
- ◯ Joyful movement
- ◯ Reading
- ◯ Gratitude
- ◯ Quiet time
- ◯ Fun time
- ◯ Mindful eating
- ◯ Goal work
- ◯ _____
- ◯ _____
- ◯ _____

How did I embrace self-compassion today?

_____
_____

What is a challenge I overcame through self-care today?

_____
_____
_____

EXERCISE

Notice the places where your body is in contact with other items.
For example, notice where your skin meets your clothes, where your
bottom meets the chair, where your feet meet the floor, and so on.
Notice places where your body is in contact with itself. For example,
notice where your lips touch, where your eyelids come together,
and so on. What is it like to pay attention to these contact points
that are normally ignored?

DAILY TRACKER

MORNING CHECK-IN

MOOD: ☺ 😄

ENERGY LEVEL: ▯ ▮ ▮

SLEEP:

FROM: _____ a.m./p.m.

TO: _____ a.m./p.m.

TOTAL: _____ hours

DAILY GOALS:

1. _____

2. _____

3. _____

AFFIRMATION OR INTENTION:

_____

_____

_____

_____

_____

_____

EVENING REFLECTION

MOOD: ☹   ☺ 😄

ENERGY LEVEL: ▯ ▮ ▮

SELF-CARE:

○ Shower/Bath   ○ Gratitude
○ Meditation   ○ Quiet time
○ Journaling   ○ Fun time
○ Joyful movement   ○ Mindful eating
○ Reading   ○ Goal work

○ _____

○ _____

○ _____

How did I embrace self-compassion today?

_____

_____

What is a challenge I overcame through self-care today?

_____

_____

REFLECTIVE PROMPT

What are the ways you can ask your friends, family, coworkers, and others to help you or support you on your self-care journey?

DAILY TRACKER

MORNING CHECK-IN

MOOD: 😞 😭 😐 😊 😆

ENERGY LEVEL: 🔋 🔋 🔋

SLEEP:

FROM: _____ a.m./p.m.

TO: _____ a.m./p.m.

TOTAL: _____ hours

DAILY GOALS:

1. _____

2. _____

3. _____

AFFIRMATION OR INTENTION:

_____

_____

_____

_____

_____

_____

EVENING REFLECTION

MOOD: 😞 😭 😐 😊 😆

ENERGY LEVEL: 🔋 🔋 🔋

SELF-CARE:

- ○ Shower/Bath
- ○ Meditation
- ○ Journaling
- ○ Joyful movement
- ○ Reading
- ○ Gratitude
- ○ Quiet time
- ○ Fun time
- ○ Mindful eating
- ○ Goal work

○ _____

○ _____

○ _____

How did I embrace self-compassion today?

_____

_____

_____

What is a challenge I overcame through self-care today?

_____

_____

_____

_____

REFLECTIVE PROMPT

When does your mind feel the clearest? How can you take advantage of these clear-minded moments to embrace more self-care?

_____

_____

_____

_____

_____

_____

_____

_____

_____

_____

_____

_____

_____

_____

_____

_____

_____

DAILY TRACKER

MORNING CHECK-IN

MOOD:

ENERGY LEVEL: 🔋 🔋 🔋

SLEEP:

FROM: _____ a.m./p.m.

TO: _____ a.m./p.m.

TOTAL: _____ hours

DAILY GOALS:

1. _____

2. _____

3. _____

AFFIRMATION OR INTENTION:

_____

_____

_____

_____

_____

EVENING REFLECTION

MOOD:

ENERGY LEVEL: 🔋 🔋 🔋

SELF-CARE:

○ Shower/Bath   ○ Gratitude
○ Meditation   ○ Quiet time
○ Journaling   ○ Fun time
○ Joyful movement ○ Mindful eating
○ Reading   ○ Goal work
○ _____
○ _____
○ _____

How did I embrace self-compassion today?

_____

_____

What is a challenge I overcame through self-care today?

_____

_____

_____

REFLECTIVE PROMPT

What are your personal warning signs of burnout? What is one thing you can do to prevent further burnout when you notice the warning signs?

DAILY TRACKER

MORNING CHECK-IN

MOOD:

ENERGY LEVEL:

SLEEP:

FROM: _____ a.m./p.m.

TO: _____ a.m./p.m.

TOTAL: _____ hours

DAILY GOALS:

1. _____

2. _____

3. _____

AFFIRMATION OR INTENTION:

_____

_____

_____

_____

_____

EVENING REFLECTION

MOOD:

ENERGY LEVEL:

SELF-CARE:

- ○ Shower/Bath
- ○ Meditation
- ○ Journaling
- ○ Joyful movement
- ○ Reading

- ○ Gratitude
- ○ Quiet time
- ○ Fun time
- ○ Mindful eating
- ○ Goal work

- ○ _____
- ○ _____
- ○ _____

How did I embrace self-compassion today?

_____

_____

_____

What is a challenge I overcame through self-care today?

_____

_____

_____

TIPS AND TRICKS

Nourish your surroundings. Find an area in your living environment that you can nourish—even if it's just a corner of a closet. Put up decor, inspirational items, or meaningful treasures that make you feel at peace. This can be a safe place for you to check in when you need a moment of calm. What items or aesthetics make you feel good?

DAILY TRACKER

MORNING CHECK-IN

MOOD:

ENERGY LEVEL: ▢ ▥ ▦

SLEEP:

FROM: _____ a.m./p.m.

TO: _____ a.m./p.m.

TOTAL: _____ hours

DAILY GOALS:

1. _____

2. _____

3. _____

AFFIRMATION OR INTENTION:

_____

_____

_____

_____

EVENING REFLECTION

MOOD: ☺ ☺ ☺

ENERGY LEVEL: ▢ ▥ ▦

SELF-CARE:

○ Shower/Bath   ○ Gratitude
○ Meditation   ○ Quiet time
○ Journaling   ○ Fun time
○ Joyful movement ○ Mindful eating
○ Reading   ○ Goal work
○ _____
○ _____
○ _____

How did I embrace self-compassion today?

_____

_____

What is a challenge I overcame through self-care today?

_____

_____

_____

REFLECTIVE PROMPT

How can you show gratitude to yourself for embracing self-care? If it is challenging for you to do so, what makes it difficult?

DAILY TRACKER

MORNING CHECK-IN

MOOD: 🙂 😄

ENERGY LEVEL: 🔋 🔋 🔋

SLEEP:

FROM: _____ a.m./p.m.

TO: _____ a.m./p.m.

TOTAL: _____ hours

DAILY GOALS:

1. _____

2. _____

3. _____

AFFIRMATION OR INTENTION:

_____

_____

_____

_____

_____

EVENING REFLECTION

MOOD: 🙂 😄

ENERGY LEVEL: 🔋 🔋 🔋

SELF-CARE:

- ◯ Shower/Bath
- ◯ Meditation
- ◯ Journaling
- ◯ Joyful movement
- ◯ Reading
- ◯ Gratitude
- ◯ Quiet time
- ◯ Fun time
- ◯ Mindful eating
- ◯ Goal work

◯ _____

◯ _____

◯ _____

How did I embrace self-compassion today?

_____

_____

_____

What is a challenge I overcame through self-care today?

_____

_____

_____

REFLECTIVE PROMPT

Where does imbalance show up in your life? How can you create more balance?

_____

_____

_____

_____

_____

_____

_____

_____

_____

_____

_____

_____

_____

_____

_____

_____

_____

DAILY TRACKER

MORNING CHECK-IN

MOOD:

ENERGY LEVEL: ▢ ▤ ▥

SLEEP:

FROM: _____ a.m./p.m.

TO: _____ a.m./p.m.

TOTAL: _____ hours

DAILY GOALS:

1. _____

2. _____

3. _____

AFFIRMATION OR INTENTION:

_____

_____

_____

_____

_____

EVENING REFLECTION

MOOD: ☺ ☺ ☺

ENERGY LEVEL: ▢ ▤ ▥

SELF-CARE:

○ Shower/Bath   ○ Gratitude
○ Meditation   ○ Quiet time
○ Journaling   ○ Fun time
○ Joyful movement   ○ Mindful eating
○ Reading   ○ Goal work

○ _____

○ _____

○ _____

How did I embrace self-compassion today?

_____

_____

_____

What is a challenge I overcame through self-care today?

_____

_____

_____

_____

REFLECTIVE PROMPT

What is your relationship to self-care and food? In what ways can you use food to nourish yourself?

DAILY TRACKER

MORNING CHECK-IN

MOOD:

ENERGY LEVEL: 🔋 🔋 🔋

SLEEP:

FROM: _____ a.m./p.m.

TO: _____ a.m./p.m.

TOTAL: _____ hours

DAILY GOALS:

1. _____
2. _____
3. _____

AFFIRMATION OR INTENTION:

_____
_____
_____
_____
_____

EVENING REFLECTION

MOOD: 😞 😭 😐 😊 😆

ENERGY LEVEL: 🔋 🔋 🔋

SELF-CARE:

- ○ Shower/Bath
- ○ Meditation
- ○ Journaling
- ○ Joyful movement
- ○ Reading
- ○ Gratitude
- ○ Quiet time
- ○ Fun time
- ○ Mindful eating
- ○ Goal work
- ○ _____
- ○ _____
- ○ _____

How did I embrace self-compassion today?

_____
_____

What is a challenge I overcame through self-care today?

_____
_____
_____

EXERCISE

Go outside and feel the fresh air on your skin. Notice the temperature and how it impacts your body. Does the sun make you warm and sweat? Does the cold make you shiver? Offer kindness to your body for attempting to adapt to the temperature. What is it like to offer your body this kindness?

_____

_____

_____

_____

_____

_____

_____

_____

_____

_____

_____

_____

_____

DAILY TRACKER

MORNING CHECK-IN

MOOD:

ENERGY LEVEL: 🔋 🔋 🔋

SLEEP:

FROM: _____ a.m./p.m.

TO: _____ a.m./p.m.

TOTAL: _____ hours

DAILY GOALS:

1. _____

2. _____

3. _____

AFFIRMATION OR INTENTION:

_____

_____

_____

_____

_____

_____

EVENING REFLECTION

MOOD:

ENERGY LEVEL: 🔋 🔋 🔋

SELF-CARE:

○ Shower/Bath   ○ Gratitude
○ Meditation   ○ Quiet time
○ Journaling   ○ Fun time
○ Joyful movement ○ Mindful eating
○ Reading   ○ Goal work

○ _____

○ _____

○ _____

How did I embrace self-compassion today?

_____

_____

What is a challenge I overcame through self-care today?

_____

_____

REFLECTIVE PROMPT

What are the ways you can communicate your needs more clearly
to others?

_____

_____

_____

_____

_____

_____

_____

_____

_____

_____

_____

_____

_____

_____

_____

_____

DAILY TRACKER

DATE: _____

S M T W TH F S

MORNING CHECK-IN

MOOD: ☺ 😄

ENERGY LEVEL: ▯ ▮ 🔋

SLEEP:

FROM: _____ a.m./p.m.

TO: _____ a.m./p.m.

TOTAL: _____ hours

DAILY GOALS:

1. _____

2. _____

3. _____

AFFIRMATION OR INTENTION:

_____

_____

_____

_____

_____

EVENING REFLECTION

MOOD: ☺ 😄

ENERGY LEVEL: ▯ ▮ 🔋

SELF-CARE:

○ Shower/Bath   ○ Gratitude
○ Meditation   ○ Quiet time
○ Journaling   ○ Fun time
○ Joyful movement   ○ Mindful eating
○ Reading   ○ Goal work
○ _____
○ _____
○ _____

How did I embrace self-compassion today?

_____

_____

What is a challenge I overcame through self-care today?

_____

_____

REFLECTIVE PROMPT

Is it challenging for you to set aside time for self-care? If so, what are the reasons, and how can you take steps to prioritize your well-being?

DAILY TRACKER

MORNING CHECK-IN

MOOD:

ENERGY LEVEL: 🔋 🔋 🔋

SLEEP:

FROM: _____ a.m./p.m.

TO: _____ a.m./p.m.

TOTAL: _____ hours

DAILY GOALS:

1. _____

2. _____

3. _____

AFFIRMATION OR INTENTION:

_____

_____

_____

_____

EVENING REFLECTION

MOOD: 😃 😄

ENERGY LEVEL: 🔋 🔋 🔋

SELF-CARE:

○ Shower/Bath   ○ Gratitude
○ Meditation   ○ Quiet time
○ Journaling   ○ Fun time
○ Joyful movement   ○ Mindful eating
○ Reading   ○ Goal work
○ _____
○ _____
○ _____

How did I embrace self-compassion today?

_____

_____

What is a challenge I overcame through self-care today?

_____

_____

_____

EXERCISE

Try box breathing (aka square breathing). Breathe in through your nose for four seconds, hold your breath for four seconds, release your breath through your mouth for four seconds, then hold your breath for four seconds. Repeat the cycle. How does it feel to consciously control your breathing in this way?

DAILY TRACKER

MORNING CHECK-IN	EVENING REFLECTION

MOOD:

MOOD:

ENERGY LEVEL: 🔋 🔋 🔋

ENERGY LEVEL: 🔋 🔋 🔋

SLEEP:

FROM: _____ a.m./p.m.

TO: _____ a.m./p.m.

TOTAL: _____ hours

DAILY GOALS:

1. _____

2. _____

3. _____

AFFIRMATION OR INTENTION:

_____

_____

_____

_____

_____

SELF-CARE:

○ Shower/Bath   ○ Gratitude
○ Meditation   ○ Quiet time
○ Journaling   ○ Fun time
○ Joyful movement ○ Mindful eating
○ Reading   ○ Goal work
○ _____
○ _____
○ _____

How did I embrace self-compassion today?

_____

_____

_____

What is a challenge I overcame through self-care today?

_____

_____

_____

REFLECTIVE PROMPT

How can you continue to cultivate a kinder relationship with yourself? In what ways can you be more understanding when you face setbacks?

DAILY TRACKER

MORNING CHECK-IN

MOOD:

ENERGY LEVEL: 🔋 🔋 🔋

SLEEP:

FROM: _____ a.m./p.m.

TO: _____ a.m./p.m.

TOTAL: _____ hours

DAILY GOALS:

1. _____

2. _____

3. _____

AFFIRMATION OR INTENTION:

_____

_____

_____

_____

_____

EVENING REFLECTION

MOOD: ☺ 😀 😆

ENERGY LEVEL: 🔋 🔋 🔋

SELF-CARE:

○ Shower/Bath   ○ Gratitude

○ Meditation   ○ Quiet time

○ Journaling   ○ Fun time

○ Joyful movement ○ Mindful eating

○ Reading   ○ Goal work

○ _____

○ _____

○ _____

How did I embrace self-compassion today?

_____

_____

What is a challenge I overcame through self-care today?

_____

_____

_____

REFLECTIVE PROMPT

What activities mentally stimulate you in a positive way?

DAILY TRACKER

MORNING CHECK-IN

MOOD:

ENERGY LEVEL: 🔋 🔋 🔋

SLEEP:

FROM: _____ a.m./p.m.

TO: _____ a.m./p.m.

TOTAL: _____ hours

DAILY GOALS:

1. _____
2. _____
3. _____

AFFIRMATION OR INTENTION:

_____
_____
_____
_____
_____

EVENING REFLECTION

MOOD: 🙁 😫 😐 🙂 😄

ENERGY LEVEL: 🔋 🔋 🔋

SELF-CARE:

- ○ Shower/Bath
- ○ Meditation
- ○ Journaling
- ○ Joyful movement
- ○ Reading
- ○ Gratitude
- ○ Quiet time
- ○ Fun time
- ○ Mindful eating
- ○ Goal work
- ○ _____
- ○ _____
- ○ _____

How did I embrace self-compassion today?

_____
_____

What is a challenge I overcame through self-care today?

_____
_____
_____

REFLECTIVE PROMPT

What can you do during your nighttime routine to foster more restful sleep? Identify the actions you can take.

DAILY TRACKER

MORNING CHECK-IN

MOOD: ☺ 😆

ENERGY LEVEL: 🔋 🔋 🔋

SLEEP:

FROM: _____ a.m./p.m.

TO: _____ a.m./p.m.

TOTAL: _____ hours

DAILY GOALS:

1. _____

2. _____

3. _____

AFFIRMATION OR INTENTION:

_____

_____

_____

_____

_____

EVENING REFLECTION

MOOD: 🙁 😐 ☺ 😆

ENERGY LEVEL: 🔋 🔋 🔋

SELF-CARE:

○ Shower/Bath   ○ Gratitude

○ Meditation   ○ Quiet time

○ Journaling   ○ Fun time

○ Joyful movement   ○ Mindful eating

○ Reading   ○ Goal work

○ _____

○ _____

○ _____

How did I embrace self-compassion today?

_____

_____

What is a challenge I overcame through self-care today?

_____

_____

EXERCISE

Sit or lie down comfortably, then gently close your eyes. Take a deep breath in, then slowly release the breath. During the release, feel your body sink into the surface below you. Take a few more deep breaths. Each time you release, feel your body sink deeper into the surface below. Feel the pull of gravity securing you to the earth. How does this connection with gravity make you feel?

DAILY TRACKER

MORNING CHECK-IN

MOOD: 🙂 😄

ENERGY LEVEL: 🔋 🔋 🔋

SLEEP:

FROM: _____ a.m./p.m.

TO: _____ a.m./p.m.

TOTAL: _____ hours

DAILY GOALS:

1. _____
2. _____
3. _____

AFFIRMATION OR INTENTION:

_____
_____
_____
_____
_____

EVENING REFLECTION

MOOD: ☹️ 🙂 😄

ENERGY LEVEL: 🔋 🔋 🔋

SELF-CARE:

○ Shower/Bath   ○ Gratitude
○ Meditation   ○ Quiet time
○ Journaling   ○ Fun time
○ Joyful movement   ○ Mindful eating
○ Reading   ○ Goal work
○ _____
○ _____
○ _____

How did I embrace self-compassion today?

_____
_____

What is a challenge I overcame through self-care today?

_____
_____
_____

REFLECTIVE PROMPT

What stops you from making your health a priority? What steps can you take to bring your health to the forefront?

DAILY TRACKER

MORNING CHECK-IN

MOOD: ☺

ENERGY LEVEL: 🔋 🔋 🔋

SLEEP:

FROM: _____ a.m./p.m.

TO: _____ a.m./p.m.

TOTAL: _____ hours

DAILY GOALS:

1. _____
2. _____
3. _____

AFFIRMATION OR INTENTION:

_____
_____
_____
_____

EVENING REFLECTION

MOOD: ☺ ☺ ☺

ENERGY LEVEL: 🔋 🔋 🔋

SELF-CARE:

○ Shower/Bath   ○ Gratitude
○ Meditation   ○ Quiet time
○ Journaling   ○ Fun time
○ Joyful movement ○ Mindful eating
○ Reading   ○ Goal work
○ _____
○ _____
○ _____

How did I embrace self-compassion today?

_____
_____
_____

What is a challenge I overcame through self-care today?

_____
_____
_____

REFLECTIVE PROMPT

Identify a time in your life when you were resilient. What parts of yourself made you resilient during that time?

DAILY TRACKER

MORNING CHECK-IN

MOOD:

ENERGY LEVEL:

SLEEP:

FROM: _____ a.m./p.m.

TO: _____ a.m./p.m.

TOTAL: _____ hours

DAILY GOALS:

1. _____

2. _____

3. _____

AFFIRMATION OR INTENTION:

_____

_____

_____

_____

_____

EVENING REFLECTION

MOOD:

ENERGY LEVEL:

SELF-CARE:

- ○ Shower/Bath
- ○ Meditation
- ○ Journaling
- ○ Joyful movement
- ○ Reading
- ○ Gratitude
- ○ Quiet time
- ○ Fun time
- ○ Mindful eating
- ○ Goal work
- ○ _____
- ○ _____
- ○ _____

How did I embrace self-compassion today?

_____

_____

What is a challenge I overcame through self-care today?

_____

_____

_____

REFLECTIVE PROMPT

Do you show up authentically with others? If not, what holds
you back?

_____

_____

_____

_____

_____

_____

_____

_____

_____

_____

_____

_____

_____

_____

_____

_____

DAILY TRACKER

MORNING CHECK-IN

MOOD: 🙂 😄

ENERGY LEVEL: ▯ ▮ ▮

SLEEP:

FROM: _____ a.m./p.m.

TO: _____ a.m./p.m.

TOTAL: _____ hours

DAILY GOALS:

1. _____

2. _____

3. _____

AFFIRMATION OR INTENTION:

_____

_____

_____

_____

_____

EVENING REFLECTION

MOOD: ☹️ 😫 😐 🙂 😄

ENERGY LEVEL: ▯ ▮ ▮

SELF-CARE:

- ○ Shower/Bath
- ○ Meditation
- ○ Journaling
- ○ Joyful movement
- ○ Reading
- ○ Gratitude
- ○ Quiet time
- ○ Fun time
- ○ Mindful eating
- ○ Goal work
- ○ _____
- ○ _____
- ○ _____

How did I embrace self-compassion today?

_____

_____

What is a challenge I overcame through self-care today?

_____

_____

_____

TIPS AND TRICKS

Invest in a fidget toy. Fidget toys are items (such as Silly Putty, stress balls, and pop spinners) you can use to easily release built-up stress during the day. What are other easy ways for your body to release tension throughout the day?

DAILY TRACKER

MORNING CHECK-IN

MOOD:

ENERGY LEVEL: 🔋 🔋 🔋

SLEEP:

FROM: _____ a.m./p.m.

TO: _____ a.m./p.m.

TOTAL: _____ hours

DAILY GOALS:

1. _____

2. _____

3. _____

AFFIRMATION OR INTENTION:

_____

_____

_____

_____

_____

EVENING REFLECTION

MOOD:

ENERGY LEVEL: 🔋 🔋 🔋

SELF-CARE:

- ○ Shower/Bath
- ○ Meditation
- ○ Journaling
- ○ Joyful movement
- ○ Reading
- ○ Gratitude
- ○ Quiet time
- ○ Fun time
- ○ Mindful eating
- ○ Goal work

○ _____

○ _____

○ _____

How did I embrace self-compassion today?

_____

_____

What is a challenge I overcame through self-care today?

_____

_____

_____

REFLECTIVE PROMPT

What is one way you showed yourself kindness today? How did it impact your mood?

_____

_____

_____

_____

_____

_____

_____

_____

_____

_____

_____

_____

_____

_____

_____

_____

_____

_____

DAILY TRACKER

MORNING CHECK-IN

MOOD: ☺

ENERGY LEVEL: 🔋 🔋 🔋

SLEEP:

FROM: _____ a.m./p.m.

TO: _____ a.m./p.m.

TOTAL: _____ hours

DAILY GOALS:

1. _____

2. _____

3. _____

AFFIRMATION OR INTENTION:

_____

_____

_____

_____

_____

EVENING REFLECTION

MOOD:

ENERGY LEVEL: 🔋 🔋 🔋

SELF-CARE:

- ○ Shower/Bath
- ○ Meditation
- ○ Journaling
- ○ Joyful movement
- ○ Reading
- ○ _____
- ○ _____
- ○ _____

- ○ Gratitude
- ○ Quiet time
- ○ Fun time
- ○ Mindful eating
- ○ Goal work

How did I embrace self-compassion today?

_____

_____

What is a challenge I overcame through self-care today?

_____

_____

REFLECTIVE PROMPT

What parts of your life lead to burnout? Identify some boundaries
you can create to prevent burnout.

DAILY TRACKER

DATE: _____

S M T W TH F S

MORNING CHECK-IN

MOOD: 😊 😆

ENERGY LEVEL: 🔋 🔋 🔋

SLEEP:

FROM: _____ a.m./p.m.

TO: _____ a.m./p.m.

TOTAL: _____ hours

DAILY GOALS:

1. _____

2. _____

3. _____

AFFIRMATION OR INTENTION:

_____

_____

_____

_____

_____

EVENING REFLECTION

MOOD: ☺ 😊 😆

ENERGY LEVEL: 🔋 🔋 🔋

SELF-CARE:

○ Shower/Bath   ○ Gratitude
○ Meditation   ○ Quiet time
○ Journaling   ○ Fun time
○ Joyful movement ○ Mindful eating
○ Reading   ○ Goal work
○ _____
○ _____
○ _____

How did I embrace self-compassion today?

_____

_____

What is a challenge I overcame through self-care today?

_____

_____

REFLECTIVE PROMPT

How often do you get to connect with nature? How does it make
you feel when you do connect?

_____

_____

_____

_____

_____

_____

_____

_____

_____

_____

_____

_____

_____

_____

DAILY TRACKER

S M T W TH F S

MORNING CHECK-IN

MOOD: ☹ 😠 😐 😊 😄

ENERGY LEVEL: 🔋 🔋 🔋

SLEEP:

FROM: _____ a.m./p.m.

TO: _____ a.m./p.m.

TOTAL: _____ hours

DAILY GOALS:

1. _____
2. _____
3. _____

AFFIRMATION OR INTENTION:

_____
_____
_____
_____
_____

EVENING REFLECTION

MOOD: ☹ 😠 😐 😊 😄

ENERGY LEVEL: 🔋 🔋 🔋

SELF-CARE:

○ Shower/Bath   ○ Gratitude
○ Meditation   ○ Quiet time
○ Journaling   ○ Fun time
○ Joyful movement   ○ Mindful eating
○ Reading   ○ Goal work
○ _____
○ _____
○ _____

How did I embrace self-compassion today?

_____
_____

What is a challenge I overcame through self-care today?

_____
_____
_____

TIPS AND TRICKS

Listen to your body. Take 10 minutes at the start or end of your day to check in with how your body feels. Notice any areas of tension or discomfort. Notice any areas of relaxation and ease. Ask yourself what your body needs. Activity? Rest? Nutrition? Medical attention? How will paying more attention to your body allow for more nourishment?

DAILY TRACKER

DATE: _____

S M T W TH F S

MORNING CHECK-IN

MOOD: ☹ 😭 😐 🙂 😄

ENERGY LEVEL: 🔋 🔋 🔋

SLEEP:

FROM: _____ a.m./p.m.

TO: _____ a.m./p.m.

TOTAL: _____ hours

DAILY GOALS:

1. _____
2. _____
3. _____

AFFIRMATION OR INTENTION:

_____

_____

_____

_____

_____

EVENING REFLECTION

MOOD: ☹ 😭 😐 🙂 😄

ENERGY LEVEL: 🔋 🔋 🔋

SELF-CARE:

○ Shower/Bath   ○ Gratitude
○ Meditation   ○ Quiet time
○ Journaling   ○ Fun time
○ Joyful movement   ○ Mindful eating
○ Reading   ○ Goal work

○ _____

○ _____

○ _____

How did I embrace self-compassion today?

_____

_____

What is a challenge I overcame through self-care today?

_____

_____

REFLECTIVE PROMPT

Are you distracted when you eat throughout the day? How can you practice more mindfulness during your meals?

DAILY TRACKER

MORNING CHECK-IN

MOOD: 🙂 😆

ENERGY LEVEL: 🔋 🔋 🔋

SLEEP:

FROM: _____ a.m./p.m.

TO: _____ a.m./p.m.

TOTAL: _____ hours

DAILY GOALS:

1. _____

2. _____

3. _____

AFFIRMATION OR INTENTION:

_____

_____

_____

_____

EVENING REFLECTION

MOOD: 😟   🙂 😆

ENERGY LEVEL: 🔋 🔋 🔋

SELF-CARE:

○ Shower/Bath   ○ Gratitude
○ Meditation   ○ Quiet time
○ Journaling   ○ Fun time
○ Joyful movement   ○ Mindful eating
○ Reading   ○ Goal work

○ _____

○ _____

○ _____

How did I embrace self-compassion today?

_____

_____

What is a challenge I overcame through self-care today?

_____

_____

REFLECTIVE PROMPT

Reflect on your gratitude recently. Are there any patterns that show up?

DAILY TRACKER

MORNING CHECK-IN

MOOD:

ENERGY LEVEL: ▯ ▮ ▮

SLEEP:

FROM: _____ a.m./p.m.

TO: _____ a.m./p.m.

TOTAL: _____ hours

DAILY GOALS:

1. _____

2. _____

3. _____

AFFIRMATION OR INTENTION:

_____

_____

_____

_____

_____

EVENING REFLECTION

MOOD:

ENERGY LEVEL: ▯ ▮ ▮

SELF-CARE:

○ Shower/Bath   ○ Gratitude
○ Meditation   ○ Quiet time
○ Journaling   ○ Fun time
○ Joyful movement   ○ Mindful eating
○ Reading   ○ Goal work

○ _____

○ _____

○ _____

How did I embrace self-compassion today?

_____

_____

_____

What is a challenge I overcame through self-care today?

_____

_____

_____

REFLECTIVE PROMPT

Do you reach out for support when you need it? How can you begin to rely more on healthy support systems?

DAILY TRACKER

MORNING CHECK-IN

MOOD: ☺ ☺ 😄

ENERGY LEVEL: ▯ ▮ ▮

SLEEP:

FROM: _____ a.m./p.m.

TO: _____ a.m./p.m.

TOTAL: _____ hours

DAILY GOALS:

1. _____

2. _____

3. _____

AFFIRMATION OR INTENTION:

_____

_____

_____

_____

_____

EVENING REFLECTION

MOOD: ☺ ☺ 😄

ENERGY LEVEL: ▯ ▮ ▮

SELF-CARE:

○ Shower/Bath   ○ Gratitude
○ Meditation   ○ Quiet time
○ Journaling   ○ Fun time
○ Joyful movement ○ Mindful eating
○ Reading   ○ Goal work

○ _____

○ _____

○ _____

How did I embrace self-compassion today?

_____

_____

What is a challenge I overcame through self-care today?

_____

_____

TIPS AND TRICKS

Don't brush aside moments of joy. Allow yourself to sit with good feelings. Notice how they make your body feel. This simple practice will allow you to more fully experience positive moments in your life. In what ways do you tend to push aside moments of happiness or minimize them?

DAILY TRACKER

MORNING CHECK-IN

MOOD: ☺ 😆

ENERGY LEVEL: 🔋 🔋 🔋

SLEEP:

FROM: _____ a.m./p.m.

TO: _____ a.m./p.m.

TOTAL: _____ hours

DAILY GOALS:

1. _____

2. _____

3. _____

AFFIRMATION OR INTENTION:

_____

_____

_____

_____

_____

_____

EVENING REFLECTION

MOOD: ☺ ☺ 😆

ENERGY LEVEL: 🔋 🔋 🔋

SELF-CARE:

- ○ Shower/Bath
- ○ Meditation
- ○ Journaling
- ○ Joyful movement
- ○ Reading
- ○ Gratitude
- ○ Quiet time
- ○ Fun time
- ○ Mindful eating
- ○ Goal work

○ _____

○ _____

○ _____

How did I embrace self-compassion today?

_____

_____

What is a challenge I overcame through self-care today?

_____

_____

REFLECTIVE PROMPT

Do you trust yourself in your self-care journey? What can you do to facilitate more trust in yourself?

DAILY TRACKER

MORNING CHECK-IN

MOOD:

ENERGY LEVEL: 🔋 🔋 🔋

SLEEP:

FROM: _____ a.m./p.m.

TO: _____ a.m./p.m.

TOTAL: _____ hours

DAILY GOALS:

1. _____
2. _____
3. _____

AFFIRMATION OR INTENTION:

_____

_____

_____

_____

_____

EVENING REFLECTION

MOOD: ☺ ☺ 😆

ENERGY LEVEL: 🔋 🔋 🔋

SELF-CARE:

○ Shower/Bath   ○ Gratitude
○ Meditation   ○ Quiet time
○ Journaling   ○ Fun time
○ Joyful movement   ○ Mindful eating
○ Reading   ○ Goal work
○ _____
○ _____
○ _____

How did I embrace self-compassion today?

_____

_____

What is a challenge I overcame through self-care today?

_____

_____

_____

REFLECTIVE PROMPT

Identify a personal value that you may not have been honoring.
What step can you take to align yourself more with this value?

DAILY TRACKER

MORNING CHECK-IN

MOOD: 🙂 😊 😄

ENERGY LEVEL: 🔋 🔋 🔋

SLEEP:

FROM: _____ a.m./p.m.

TO: _____ a.m./p.m.

TOTAL: _____ hours

DAILY GOALS:

1. _____

2. _____

3. _____

AFFIRMATION OR INTENTION:

_____

_____

_____

_____

_____

EVENING REFLECTION

MOOD: 🙂 😄

ENERGY LEVEL: 🔋 🔋 🔋

SELF-CARE:

○ Shower/Bath	○ Gratitude
○ Meditation	○ Quiet time
○ Journaling	○ Fun time
○ Joyful movement	○ Mindful eating
○ Reading	○ Goal work

○ _____

○ _____

○ _____

How did I embrace self-compassion today?

_____

_____

What is a challenge I overcame through self-care today?

_____

_____

REFLECTIVE PROMPT

What is something that can instantly disrupt a good mood for you?
The next time this happens, how can you embrace self-care?

_____

_____

_____

_____

_____

_____

_____

_____

_____

_____

_____

_____

_____

_____

_____

_____

_____

_____

DAILY TRACKER

MORNING CHECK-IN

MOOD: ☺ ☺

ENERGY LEVEL: ▢ ▤ ▥

SLEEP:

FROM: _____ a.m./p.m.

TO: _____ a.m./p.m.

TOTAL: _____ hours

DAILY GOALS:

1. _____
2. _____
3. _____

AFFIRMATION OR INTENTION:

_____
_____
_____
_____
_____

EVENING REFLECTION

MOOD: ☺ ☺ ☺

ENERGY LEVEL: ▢ ▤ ▥

SELF-CARE:

○ Shower/Bath   ○ Gratitude
○ Meditation   ○ Quiet time
○ Journaling   ○ Fun time
○ Joyful movement   ○ Mindful eating
○ Reading   ○ Goal work
○ _____
○ _____
○ _____

How did I embrace self-compassion today?

_____
_____
_____

What is a challenge I overcame through self-care today?

_____
_____
_____

EXERCISE

Engage in supportive touch. Place your hand over your heart. Close your eyes and feel into this kind gesture. Notice the warmth. Next, hold your face in your hands. Notice the sensations that arise. Practice other forms of supportive touch that feel good to you. What is it like to touch yourself in a caring way?

DAILY TRACKER

MORNING CHECK-IN

MOOD: 😄

ENERGY LEVEL: 🔋 🔋 🔋

SLEEP:

FROM: _____ a.m./p.m.

TO: _____ a.m./p.m.

TOTAL: _____ hours

DAILY GOALS:

1. _____
2. _____
3. _____

AFFIRMATION OR INTENTION:

_____

_____

_____

_____

_____

EVENING REFLECTION

MOOD: ☹️ 😠 😐 🙂 😄

ENERGY LEVEL: 🔋 🔋 🔋

SELF-CARE:

- ○ Shower/Bath
- ○ Meditation
- ○ Journaling
- ○ Joyful movement
- ○ Reading
- ○ Gratitude
- ○ Quiet time
- ○ Fun time
- ○ Mindful eating
- ○ Goal work
- ○ _____
- ○ _____
- ○ _____

How did I embrace self-compassion today?

_____

_____

What is a challenge I overcame through self-care today?

_____

_____

REFLECTIVE PROMPT

What inspires you on this journey of self-care and growth?

_____

_____

_____

_____

_____

_____

_____

_____

_____

_____

_____

_____

_____

_____

_____

_____

_____

_____

_____

_____

DAILY TRACKER

DATE: _____

S M T W TH F S

MORNING CHECK-IN

MOOD:

ENERGY LEVEL: 🔋 🔋 🔋

SLEEP:

FROM: _____ a.m./p.m.

TO: _____ a.m./p.m.

TOTAL: _____ hours

DAILY GOALS:

1. _____

2. _____

3. _____

AFFIRMATION OR INTENTION:

_____

_____

_____

_____

_____

EVENING REFLECTION

MOOD:

ENERGY LEVEL: 🔋 🔋 🔋

SELF-CARE:

○ Shower/Bath   ○ Gratitude

○ Meditation   ○ Quiet time

○ Journaling   ○ Fun time

○ Joyful movement   ○ Mindful eating

○ Reading   ○ Goal work

○ _____

○ _____

○ _____

How did I embrace self-compassion today?

_____

_____

_____

What is a challenge I overcame through self-care today?

_____

_____

_____

REFLECTIVE PROMPT

What would you share with your childhood self to start them on their self-care journey?

_____

_____

_____

_____

_____

_____

_____

_____

_____

_____

_____

_____

_____

_____

_____

_____

_____

DAILY TRACKER

MORNING CHECK-IN	EVENING REFLECTION

MOOD: ☺ 😄   *MOOD:* ☹ 😖 😐 ☺ 😄

ENERGY LEVEL: 🔋 🔋 🔋   *ENERGY LEVEL:* 🔋 🔋 🔋

SLEEP:

FROM: _____ a.m./p.m.

TO: _____ a.m./p.m.

TOTAL: _____ hours

DAILY GOALS:

1. _____

2. _____

3. _____

AFFIRMATION OR INTENTION:

_____

_____

_____

_____

_____

SELF-CARE:

○ Shower/Bath   ○ Gratitude

○ Meditation   ○ Quiet time

○ Journaling   ○ Fun time

○ Joyful movement ○ Mindful eating

○ Reading   ○ Goal work

○ _____

○ _____

○ _____

How did I embrace self-compassion today?

_____

_____

What is a challenge I overcame through self-care today?

_____

_____

REFLECTIVE PROMPT

Do you let yourself celebrate your wins or do you brush them aside? How can you make more room for celebration in your life?

DAILY TRACKER

MORNING CHECK-IN

MOOD:

ENERGY LEVEL: 🔋 🔋 🔋

SLEEP:

FROM: _____ a.m./p.m.

TO: _____ a.m./p.m.

TOTAL: _____ hours

DAILY GOALS:

1. _____

2. _____

3. _____

AFFIRMATION OR INTENTION:

_____

_____

_____

_____

_____

EVENING REFLECTION

MOOD: 🙂 😊 😄

ENERGY LEVEL: 🔋 🔋 🔋

SELF-CARE:

- ⭕ Shower/Bath
- ⭕ Meditation
- ⭕ Journaling
- ⭕ Joyful movement
- ⭕ Reading
- ⭕ Gratitude
- ⭕ Quiet time
- ⭕ Fun time
- ⭕ Mindful eating
- ⭕ Goal work
- ⭕ _____
- ⭕ _____
- ⭕ _____

How did I embrace self-compassion today?

_____

_____

What is a challenge I overcame through self-care today?

_____

_____

_____

EXERCISE

Think of a person with whom you feel safe or a place that makes you feel safe. Close your eyes and envision that person or place in great detail. Notice what the person or place looks like, sounds like, feels like, and smells like. Imagine that this person or place is inviting you into their/its safety. Then offer gratitude to this person or place. How does it feel to connect with this person or place in your mind?

DAILY TRACKER

MORNING CHECK-IN

MOOD:

ENERGY LEVEL: 🔋 🔋 🔋

SLEEP:

FROM: _____ a.m./p.m.

TO: _____ a.m./p.m.

TOTAL: _____ hours

DAILY GOALS:

1. _____

2. _____

3. _____

AFFIRMATION OR INTENTION:

_____

_____

_____

_____

_____

_____

EVENING REFLECTION

MOOD: ☺ ☺ ☺

ENERGY LEVEL: 🔋 🔋 🔋

SELF-CARE:

○ Shower/Bath   ○ Gratitude
○ Meditation   ○ Quiet time
○ Journaling   ○ Fun time
○ Joyful movement   ○ Mindful eating
○ Reading   ○ Goal work
○ _____
○ _____
○ _____

How did I embrace self-compassion today?

_____

_____

What is a challenge I overcame through self-care today?

_____

_____

_____

REFLECTIVE PROMPT

In what ways do you struggle to advocate for your self-care? How can you begin to start saying no to things and focus on yourself?

DAILY TRACKER

MORNING CHECK-IN

MOOD: ☺ 😄

ENERGY LEVEL: 🔋 🔋 🔋

SLEEP:

FROM: _____ a.m./p.m.

TO: _____ a.m./p.m.

TOTAL: _____ hours

DAILY GOALS:

1. _____
2. _____
3. _____

AFFIRMATION OR INTENTION:

_____
_____
_____
_____
_____

EVENING REFLECTION

MOOD: ☹   ☺ 😄

ENERGY LEVEL: 🔋 🔋 🔋

SELF-CARE:

○ Shower/Bath   ○ Gratitude
○ Meditation   ○ Quiet time
○ Journaling   ○ Fun time
○ Joyful movement ○ Mindful eating
○ Reading   ○ Goal work
○ _____
○ _____
○ _____

How did I embrace self-compassion today?

_____
_____

What is a challenge I overcame through self-care today?

_____
_____
_____

REFLECTIVE PROMPT

What challenges did you face today, and what did you do to get through them?

_____

_____

_____

_____

_____

_____

_____

_____

_____

_____

_____

_____

_____

_____

_____

DAILY TRACKER

DATE: _____

S M T W TH F S

MORNING CHECK-IN

MOOD: ☺ 😄

ENERGY LEVEL: 🔋 🔋 🔋

SLEEP:

FROM: _____ a.m./p.m.

TO: _____ a.m./p.m.

TOTAL: _____ hours

DAILY GOALS:

1. _____

2. _____

3. _____

AFFIRMATION OR INTENTION:

_____

_____

_____

_____

_____

EVENING REFLECTION

MOOD: ☺ ☺ 😄

ENERGY LEVEL: 🔋 🔋 🔋

SELF-CARE:

○ Shower/Bath   ○ Gratitude

○ Meditation   ○ Quiet time

○ Journaling   ○ Fun time

○ Joyful movement   ○ Mindful eating

○ Reading   ○ Goal work

○ _____

○ _____

○ _____

How did I embrace self-compassion today?

_____

_____

What is a challenge I overcame through self-care today?

_____

_____

_____

REFLECTIVE PROMPT

What are you proud of yourself for? What accomplishments have you achieved?

_____

_____

_____

_____

_____

_____

_____

_____

_____

_____

_____

_____

_____

_____

_____

_____

DAILY TRACKER

DATE: _____

S M T W TH F S

MORNING CHECK-IN

MOOD:

ENERGY LEVEL: 🔋 🔋 🔋

SLEEP:

FROM: _____ a.m./p.m.

TO: _____ a.m./p.m.

TOTAL: _____ hours

DAILY GOALS:

1. _____

2. _____

3. _____

AFFIRMATION OR INTENTION:

_____

_____

_____

_____

_____

EVENING REFLECTION

MOOD: ☺ ☺ ☺

ENERGY LEVEL: 🔋 🔋 🔋

SELF-CARE:

○ Shower/Bath   ○ Gratitude

○ Meditation   ○ Quiet time

○ Journaling   ○ Fun time

○ Joyful movement   ○ Mindful eating

○ Reading   ○ Goal work

○ _____

○ _____

○ _____

How did I embrace self-compassion today?

_____

_____

What is a challenge I overcame through self-care today?

_____

_____

_____

TIPS AND TRICKS

On your phone, or another timing device, set a few timers to alert you across different points of the day (e.g., morning, afternoon, night). When the alarm goes off, check in with your mood. Then identify what may be impacting your mood. This checking in helps facilitate more mindfulness around your emotions. How can being aware of your emotions throughout the day lead to more self-care?

DAILY TRACKER

MORNING CHECK-IN

MOOD: ☺ 😄

ENERGY LEVEL: ▢ ▤ ▤

SLEEP:

FROM: _____ a.m./p.m.

TO: _____ a.m./p.m.

TOTAL: _____ hours

DAILY GOALS:

1. _____
2. _____
3. _____

AFFIRMATION OR INTENTION:

_____

_____

_____

_____

_____

EVENING REFLECTION

MOOD: 😞   😄

ENERGY LEVEL: ▢ ▤ ▤

SELF-CARE:

○ Shower/Bath   ○ Gratitude
○ Meditation   ○ Quiet time
○ Journaling   ○ Fun time
○ Joyful movement   ○ Mindful eating
○ Reading   ○ Goal work
○ _____
○ _____
○ _____

How did I embrace self-compassion today?

_____

_____

What is a challenge I overcame through self-care today?

_____

_____

_____

REFLECTIVE PROMPT

Do you spend time with yourself alone? If not, what holds you back from doing so?

_____

_____

_____

_____

_____

_____

_____

_____

_____

_____

_____

_____

_____

_____

_____

_____

DAILY TRACKER

DATE: _____
S M T W TH F S

MORNING CHECK-IN

MOOD:

ENERGY LEVEL: 🔋 🔋 🔋

SLEEP:

FROM: _____ a.m./p.m.

TO: _____ a.m./p.m.

TOTAL: _____ hours

DAILY GOALS:

1. _____

2. _____

3. _____

AFFIRMATION OR INTENTION:

_____

_____

_____

_____

EVENING REFLECTION

MOOD: 🙂 😆

ENERGY LEVEL: 🔋 🔋 🔋

SELF-CARE:

- ○ Shower/Bath
- ○ Meditation
- ○ Journaling
- ○ Joyful movement
- ○ Reading
- ○ Gratitude
- ○ Quiet time
- ○ Fun time
- ○ Mindful eating
- ○ Goal work
- ○ _____
- ○ _____
- ○ _____

How did I embrace self-compassion today?

_____

_____

What is a challenge I overcame through self-care today?

_____

_____

REFLECTIVE PROMPT

What is something you have been holding against yourself? What can you do to forgive yourself?

_____

_____

_____

_____

_____

_____

_____

_____

_____

_____

_____

_____

_____

_____

_____

_____

_____

DAILY TRACKER

MORNING CHECK-IN

MOOD:

ENERGY LEVEL:

SLEEP:

FROM: _____ a.m./p.m.

TO: _____ a.m./p.m.

TOTAL: _____ hours

DAILY GOALS:

1. _____

2. _____

3. _____

AFFIRMATION OR INTENTION:

_____

_____

_____

_____

_____

EVENING REFLECTION

MOOD:

ENERGY LEVEL:

SELF-CARE:

- ○ Shower/Bath
- ○ Meditation
- ○ Journaling
- ○ Joyful movement
- ○ Reading
- ○ Gratitude
- ○ Quiet time
- ○ Fun time
- ○ Mindful eating
- ○ Goal work

○ _____

○ _____

○ _____

How did I embrace self-compassion today?

_____

_____

_____

What is a challenge I overcame through self-care today?

_____

_____

_____

REFLECTIVE PROMPT

How can you meet your flaws with compassion? What can you do to show yourself grace in moments of imperfection?

DAILY TRACKER

MORNING CHECK-IN

EVENING REFLECTION

MOOD: 😆

ENERGY LEVEL: 🔋 🔋 🔋

SLEEP:

FROM: _____ a.m./p.m.

TO: _____ a.m./p.m.

TOTAL: _____ hours

DAILY GOALS:

1. _____

2. _____

3. _____

AFFIRMATION OR INTENTION:

_____

_____

_____

_____

_____

MOOD: 🙂 😀 😆

ENERGY LEVEL: 🔋 🔋 🔋

SELF-CARE:

○ Shower/Bath   ○ Gratitude
○ Meditation   ○ Quiet time
○ Journaling   ○ Fun time
○ Joyful movement ○ Mindful eating
○ Reading   ○ Goal work
○ _____
○ _____
○ _____

How did I embrace self-compassion today?

_____

_____

What is a challenge I overcame through self-care today?

_____

_____

_____

EXERCISE

Engage all of your five senses during your next meal. Notice what your food looks like, what it smells like, what it sounds like, and what it tastes like. Notice how it feels to touch it and feel its presence in your mouth. After doing so, reflect on your experience below.

DAILY TRACKER

MORNING CHECK-IN

MOOD:

ENERGY LEVEL: 🔋 🔋 🔋

SLEEP:

FROM: _____a.m./p.m.

TO: _____a.m./p.m.

TOTAL: _____ hours

DAILY GOALS:

1. _____

2. _____

3. _____

AFFIRMATION OR INTENTION:

_____

_____

_____

_____

_____

EVENING REFLECTION

MOOD:

ENERGY LEVEL: 🔋 🔋 🔋

SELF-CARE:

- ○ Shower/Bath
- ○ Meditation
- ○ Journaling
- ○ Joyful movement
- ○ Reading
- ○ Gratitude
- ○ Quiet time
- ○ Fun time
- ○ Mindful eating
- ○ Goal work

- ○ _____
- ○ _____
- ○ _____

How did I embrace self-compassion today?

_____

_____

What is a challenge I overcame through self-care today?

_____

_____

_____

REFLECTIVE PROMPT

What activities do you waste the most time on? What can you do to use this time more wisely?

_____

_____

_____

_____

_____

_____

_____

_____

_____

_____

_____

_____

_____

_____

_____

_____

_____

_____

DAILY TRACKER

MORNING CHECK-IN

MOOD:

ENERGY LEVEL: 🔋 🔋 🔋

SLEEP:

FROM: _____ a.m./p.m.

TO: _____ a.m./p.m.

TOTAL: _____ hours

DAILY GOALS:

1. _____

2. _____

3. _____

AFFIRMATION OR INTENTION:

_____

_____

_____

_____

_____

EVENING REFLECTION

MOOD:

ENERGY LEVEL: 🔋 🔋 🔋

SELF-CARE:

○ Shower/Bath   ○ Gratitude
○ Meditation   ○ Quiet time
○ Journaling   ○ Fun time
○ Joyful movement   ○ Mindful eating
○ Reading   ○ Goal work
○ _____
○ _____
○ _____

How did I embrace self-compassion today?

_____

_____

_____

What is a challenge I overcame through self-care today?

_____

_____

_____

_____

REFLECTIVE PROMPT

Identify a time when you felt more confident in yourself. What impacted this greater confidence?

_____

_____

_____

_____

_____

_____

_____

_____

_____

_____

_____

_____

_____

_____

_____

_____

_____

DAILY TRACKER

MORNING CHECK-IN

MOOD:

ENERGY LEVEL: ▯ ▮ ▮

SLEEP:

FROM: _____ a.m./p.m.

TO: _____ a.m./p.m.

TOTAL: _____ hours

DAILY GOALS:

1. _____

2. _____

3. _____

AFFIRMATION OR INTENTION:

_____

_____

_____

_____

_____

EVENING REFLECTION

MOOD: ☹ 😭 😐 🙂 😄

ENERGY LEVEL: ▯ ▮ ▮

SELF-CARE:

○ Shower/Bath   ○ Gratitude
○ Meditation   ○ Quiet time
○ Journaling   ○ Fun time
○ Joyful movement   ○ Mindful eating
○ Reading   ○ Goal work
○ _____
○ _____
○ _____

How did I embrace self-compassion today?

_____

_____

_____

What is a challenge I overcame through self-care today?

_____

_____

_____

TIPS AND TRICKS

Spend some time before going to bed without electronic devices—anywhere from 30 minutes to two hours. Notice how it feels to spend time without them. Notice if it changes your quality of sleep. Then reflect on your experience below.

DAILY TRACKER

MORNING CHECK-IN

MOOD: ☺ ☺ ☺

ENERGY LEVEL: 🔋 🔋 🔋

SLEEP:

FROM: _____ a.m./p.m.

TO: _____ a.m./p.m.

TOTAL: _____ hours

DAILY GOALS:

1. _____

2. _____

3. _____

AFFIRMATION OR INTENTION:

_____

_____

_____

_____

EVENING REFLECTION

MOOD: ☹ ☺ ☺ ☺

ENERGY LEVEL: 🔋 🔋 🔋

SELF-CARE:

- ○ Shower/Bath
- ○ Meditation
- ○ Journaling
- ○ Joyful movement
- ○ Reading
- ○ Gratitude
- ○ Quiet time
- ○ Fun time
- ○ Mindful eating
- ○ Goal work

○ _____

○ _____

○ _____

How did I embrace self-compassion today?

_____

_____

_____

What is a challenge I overcame through self-care today?

_____

_____

_____

REFLECTIVE PROMPT

When does life feel the most magical for you? What factors play a role in this?

_____

_____

_____

_____

_____

_____

_____

_____

_____

_____

_____

_____

_____

_____

_____

_____

_____

DAILY TRACKER

MORNING CHECK-IN

MOOD:

ENERGY LEVEL:

SLEEP:

FROM: _____ a.m./p.m.

TO: _____ a.m./p.m.

TOTAL: _____ hours

DAILY GOALS:

1. _____

2. _____

3. _____

AFFIRMATION OR INTENTION:

_____

_____

_____

_____

_____

EVENING REFLECTION

MOOD:

ENERGY LEVEL:

SELF-CARE:

○ Shower/Bath   ○ Gratitude

○ Meditation   ○ Quiet time

○ Journaling   ○ Fun time

○ Joyful movement   ○ Mindful eating

○ Reading   ○ Goal work

○ _____

○ _____

○ _____

How did I embrace self-compassion today?

_____

_____

What is a challenge I overcame through self-care today?

_____

_____

REFLECTIVE PROMPT

Do you take care of your living space? What is one way to bring more care to your living environment?

DAILY TRACKER

MORNING CHECK-IN

MOOD: 😆

ENERGY LEVEL: 🔋 🔋 🔋

SLEEP:

FROM: _____ a.m./p.m.

TO: _____ a.m./p.m.

TOTAL: _____ hours

DAILY GOALS:

1. _____

2. _____

3. _____

AFFIRMATION OR INTENTION:

_____

_____

_____

_____

_____

EVENING REFLECTION

MOOD: 🙂 😊 😆

ENERGY LEVEL: 🔋 🔋 🔋

SELF-CARE:

○ Shower/Bath   ○ Gratitude
○ Meditation   ○ Quiet time
○ Journaling   ○ Fun time
○ Joyful movement   ○ Mindful eating
○ Reading   ○ Goal work
○ _____
○ _____
○ _____

How did I embrace self-compassion today?

_____

_____

What is a challenge I overcame through self-care today?

_____

_____

_____

EXERCISE

Check in with your current mood. Then get rid of any distractions and put on your favorite feel-good song. Listen to the different instruments, the melody, and the lyrics. Feel free to sing along or move your body if you feel inspired. After the song is over, check in with your mood again. How did your mood shift after listening to this song?

DAILY TRACKER

MORNING CHECK-IN

MOOD:

ENERGY LEVEL:

SLEEP:

FROM: _____ a.m./p.m.

TO: _____ a.m./p.m.

TOTAL: _____ hours

DAILY GOALS:

1. _____

2. _____

3. _____

AFFIRMATION OR INTENTION:

_____

_____

_____

_____

_____

EVENING REFLECTION

MOOD:

ENERGY LEVEL:

SELF-CARE:

○ Shower/Bath   ○ Gratitude

○ Meditation   ○ Quiet time

○ Journaling   ○ Fun time

○ Joyful movement ○ Mindful eating

○ Reading   ○ Goal work

○ _____

○ _____

○ _____

How did I embrace self-compassion today?

_____

_____

_____

What is a challenge I overcame through self-care today?

_____

_____

_____

REFLECTIVE PROMPT

What is one thing that made you smile today? Why do you think it had this effect on you?

DAILY TRACKER

MORNING CHECK-IN

MOOD:

ENERGY LEVEL: 🔋 🔋 🔋

SLEEP:

FROM: _____ a.m./p.m.

TO: _____ a.m./p.m.

TOTAL: _____ hours

DAILY GOALS:

1. _____

2. _____

3. _____

AFFIRMATION OR INTENTION:

_____

_____

_____

_____

_____

EVENING REFLECTION

MOOD:

ENERGY LEVEL: 🔋 🔋 🔋

SELF-CARE:

○ Shower/Bath   ○ Gratitude

○ Meditation   ○ Quiet time

○ Journaling   ○ Fun time

○ Joyful movement   ○ Mindful eating

○ Reading   ○ Goal work

○ _____

○ _____

○ _____

How did I embrace self-compassion today?

_____

_____

What is a challenge I overcame through self-care today?

_____

_____

_____

REFLECTIVE PROMPT

Rest is productive, as it restores your energy. What restful activities are most restorative for you?

_____

_____

_____

_____

_____

_____

_____

_____

_____

_____

_____

_____

_____

_____

_____

_____

DAILY TRACKER

MORNING CHECK-IN

MOOD:

ENERGY LEVEL: 🔋🔋🔋

SLEEP:

FROM: _____ a.m./p.m.

TO: _____ a.m./p.m.

TOTAL: _____ hours

DAILY GOALS:

1. _____

2. _____

3. _____

AFFIRMATION OR INTENTION:

_____

_____

_____

_____

_____

EVENING REFLECTION

MOOD:

ENERGY LEVEL: 🔋🔋🔋

SELF-CARE:

- ○ Shower/Bath
- ○ Meditation
- ○ Journaling
- ○ Joyful movement
- ○ Reading
- ○ Gratitude
- ○ Quiet time
- ○ Fun time
- ○ Mindful eating
- ○ Goal work

○ _____

○ _____

○ _____

How did I embrace self-compassion today?

_____

_____

What is a challenge I overcame through self-care today?

_____

_____

REFLECTIVE PROMPT

How can you foster more flexibility in your life? Why is it important
to do so?

DAILY TRACKER

MORNING CHECK-IN

MOOD:

ENERGY LEVEL: 🔋 🔋 🔋

SLEEP:

FROM: _____ a.m./p.m.

TO: _____ a.m./p.m.

TOTAL: _____ hours

DAILY GOALS:

1. _____

2. _____

3. _____

AFFIRMATION OR INTENTION:

_____

_____

_____

_____

_____

EVENING REFLECTION

MOOD:

ENERGY LEVEL: 🔋 🔋 🔋

SELF-CARE:

○ Shower/Bath   ○ Gratitude
○ Meditation   ○ Quiet time
○ Journaling   ○ Fun time
○ Joyful movement ○ Mindful eating
○ Reading   ○ Goal work
○ _____
○ _____
○ _____

How did I embrace self-compassion today?

_____

_____

What is a challenge I overcame through self-care today?

_____

_____

_____

TIPS AND TRICKS

When you are being hard on yourself, have a mental dialogue between your inner critic voice and your self-compassionate voice. Identify the self-critical thought you are having, then embrace self-compassion through positive self-talk. How can you show yourself more kindness and understanding in those moments?

DAILY TRACKER

MORNING CHECK-IN

MOOD:

ENERGY LEVEL: 🔋 🔋 🔋

SLEEP:

FROM: _____ a.m./p.m.

TO: _____ a.m./p.m.

TOTAL: _____ hours

DAILY GOALS:

1. _____

2. _____

3. _____

AFFIRMATION OR INTENTION:

_____

_____

_____

_____

_____

EVENING REFLECTION

MOOD:

ENERGY LEVEL: 🔋 🔋 🔋

SELF-CARE:

○ Shower/Bath   ○ Gratitude
○ Meditation   ○ Quiet time
○ Journaling   ○ Fun time
○ Joyful movement   ○ Mindful eating
○ Reading   ○ Goal work
○ _____
○ _____
○ _____

How did I embrace self-compassion today?

_____

_____

What is a challenge I overcame through self-care today?

_____

_____

_____

REFLECTIVE PROMPT

What is something you are genuinely looking forward to? What are the reasons why?

DAILY TRACKER

MORNING CHECK-IN

EVENING REFLECTION

MOOD: ☹ 😭 😐 🙂 😄

ENERGY LEVEL: 🔋 🔋 🔋

SLEEP:

FROM: _____ a.m./p.m.

TO: _____ a.m./p.m.

TOTAL: _____ hours

DAILY GOALS:

1. _____

2. _____

3. _____

AFFIRMATION OR INTENTION:

_____

_____

_____

_____

_____

MOOD: ☹ 😭 😐 🙂 😄

ENERGY LEVEL: 🔋 🔋 🔋

SELF-CARE:

○ Shower/Bath   ○ Gratitude
○ Meditation   ○ Quiet time
○ Journaling   ○ Fun time
○ Joyful movement   ○ Mindful eating
○ Reading   ○ Goal work
○ _____
○ _____
○ _____

How did I embrace self-compassion today?

_____

_____

What is a challenge I overcame through self-care today?

_____

_____

_____

REFLECTIVE PROMPT

How has tracking your self-care impacted your self-care journey?
Identify any setbacks or accomplishments you have experienced
thus far.

_____

_____

_____

_____

_____

_____

_____

_____

_____

_____

_____

_____

_____

_____

_____

_____

_____

Resources

A Year of Self-Care: Daily Practices and Inspiration for Caring for Yourself by Dr. Zoe Shaw

A Year of Self-Care Journal: 52 Weeks to Cultivate Positivity & Joy by Allison Task, MS, PCC

The Positive Thinking Workbook: Quiet Your Inner Critic and Build a Strong Foundation for a Positive Mindset by Alexa Brand, MS, LMFT

The Self-Care Prescription: Powerful Solutions to Manage Stress, Reduce Anxiety and Increase Well-Being by Robyn L. Gobin, PhD

References

Brach, Tara. *Radical Compassion: Learning to Love Yourself and Your World with the Practice of RAIN.* New York: Viking, 2019.

Clear, James. *Atomic Habits: An Easy & Proven Way to Build Good Habits & Break Bad Ones.* New York: Avery, 2018.

Hanh, Thich Nhat. *The Miracle of Mindfulness: An Introduction to the Practice of Meditation.* Boston: Beacon Press, 1987.

Huber, Cheri. *I Don't Want to, I Don't Feel Like It: How Resistance Controls Your Life and What to Do About It.* Murphys, CA: Keep It Simple Books, 2013.

Riegel, Barbara, Sandra B. Dunbar, Donna Fitzsimons, Kenneth E. Freedland, Christopher S. Lee, Sandy Middleton, Anna Stromberg, Ercole Vellone, David E. Webber, and Tiny Jaarsma. "Self-Care Research: Where Are We Now? Where Are We Going?" *International Journal of Nursing Studies* 116 (April 2021): 103402 .doi.org/10.1016/j.ijnurstu.2019.103402.

Siegel, Daniel J. *Aware: The Science and Practice of Presence.* Carlton North, Australia: Scribe, 2018.

Taylor, Sonya Renee. *The Body Is Not an Apology: The Power of Radical Self-Love.* Oakland, CA: Berrett-Koehler, 2021.

Acknowledgments

Thank you to J for your infinite support and being my secure base. Thank you to C, G, and L for nurturing me into the resilient woman I am today. And thank you to my editor, Eun, for your patience and kindness.

About the Author

 Alexa Brand (she/her), LMFT, is a licensed marriage and family therapist, self-compassion expert, and author based in Los Angeles, California. For more information about Alexa, visit SoulCompassion.com.

CPSIA information can be obtained
at www.ICGtesting.com
Printed in the USA
JSHW030253150322
23789JS00001B/1